Beyond the Blue Door

poetry and pros

of

J D Roland

To Mereth's;
Don
with my
Appreciation

- 2 -

dedications

Mom & Dad
thank you for a gifted life

…

Jim & Cindge
through thick and thin

…

myspace friends
my sounding board

----

all works contained within these pages are the sole
property of JD Roland

ISBN 978-0-6152-1178-7

Under the protection of
Sun – Dial Publishing
a Nuttall Company

©2008/jdr

Table of Contents

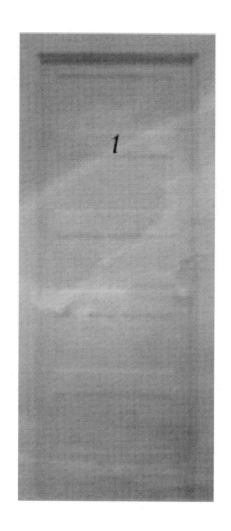

1

in daylight's dawning hours, when all else seems to sleep, I find my pen it's mightiest from slumber's wonderings.

Morning Blue

I drift within the late night shallows,
caught in tides of unending turmoil,
vigor driven like a mad parable,
busting until the pain over takes me.

I collapse before my guilded gate,
let through this barrier of self-pity,
standing back to regroup its latch
drops, my barricade flies from it's hinges.

release scatters my emptiness into the
never-ending, in twisting turning redemption,
only to fall again into self-loathing,
again, I take up arms with catapult extended
letting loose my dignity.

I am only here to influence and be influenced,
all other goals are but emotions lost on
the winds of change, I kneel before the eye
of acceptance and ask to be blind to man's
unending folly.

my neighbor is my reflection, my enemy
but a glimpse into my former, for me to
judge I must look past my calm and become
my enemy, become my self-loathing, tread
upon loose sand.

I pass beyond self-doubt into self-awareness,
judgment ceases to capture my doubt, the vines
of understanding reach beyond my awakening
into the spheres of knowledge and truth,
I wake to a beautiful day, somewhere
Beyond the Blue Door.

Butterfly Window

most days, the simple things go unnoticed,
it's not intentional, just lost to routine,
like the lamp on the end table, I placed it
there thinking, what a great place for a lamp.

now I hardly take notice, it's just a lamp,
I buttered my toast this morning, the crumbs
still lay scattered, a minor eye-sore, I will
give them my attention as they multiply.

a picture may hang off center for days,
yet I miss the ashtray and quickly maneuver
the remains to their intended target, it's beyond
me why certain things take precedence.

every time I open the back door it cries out
as though it was never meant to move,
I have a spray that would ease its pain
but then this would interrupt my destination.

every window save one could easily
be used as a note pad or seen as an
artist's foggy day interpretation,
I must admit to a streak of procrastination.

the one window omitted from this avoidance
looks out from where I write and create,
a gateway to all things possible, a kaleidoscope
which holds all life's wonderment.

I clean it diligently and without fail,
it remains, my butterfly window.

Seasons

we are thrust into the future while
our thoughts, comfortably, dwell in
the past, constantly undone by the
present, in never ending loops.

we talk of winter as though a dagger
has split the still air and pierced us to
the core, a cleansing of all that has past,
a chance to pause, reflect, rebuild.

reborn by the luster of spring, greens
and pastel pedals replace the aging grey,
crystal shards replaced by sparkling
brooks, such magic passes too quickly.

the kaleidoscope turns to summer,
heavens open the majestic splendor,
action producing connection,
connection replacing solitude.

all is well as fall sheds its skin,
the wilted and used tumble to the ground,
established, embedded in a year that
has past, descending toward a new beginning.

we search for new epitaphs,
the pendulum sweeps without pause,
unceasing, unrelenting crash and fade,
chipping away at eternity.

A Morning Cleanse

I sometimes walk to clear
my thoughts,
unconcerned with physical benefit,
relaxed in casual confidence.

I'm not obsessed by pace,
rushing along hips rotating,
clutching midget sized weights,
my beginning mingling with
destination.

no, for me it's the solitude I seek,
as if some alien encounter had
sterilized my world while I slept,
leaving behind all but the human race.

the introduction of a new day,
serene, pensive,
without flaw,
the air crisp like shattered glass,
my senses collectively acute.

the first three blocks a residential maze,
wanna-be watch dogs announce my presence,
wake up neighborhood,
they insist,
take notice of this intruder.

exiting the last signs of civilized intrusion,
nature's wonderland opens before me,
the dew laden fodder clings knee high,
I reach out and touch my isolation.

clearing my head of the day to
day tragedies of a world in turmoil,
opening my mind to free thinking,
gone are the petty self indignations.

as the sun peaks over the eastern skyline
turning the cosmos into pastel amazement
I become one,
in the moment,
no before,
no after,

A Sunday Rain

That day it rained I didn't see the sun, not that it could lay sway to my indifference. In so many ways I think myself nocturnal, drifting through days, dancing by night, my days are for the gathering in, my nights are my conclusions.

I thought of challenging Steinbeck to a walk among the unfortunate but felt it would only feed my melancholy. Possibly, Beethoven could have ignited my passion to write. Not in that moment, I had little use for writing in that moment.

As I gazed out into the Sunday rain I found myself counting raindrops, the futility seemed to comfort me. The drops exploding at journeys end, creating anarchy upon the blacktop, running to nowhere like commuters at rush hour.

I looked deeper into the cascading curtain, past the physical, beyond its nourishment, past the city streets, across the rolling hills, journeying to the very peak of imagination where the nameless leave their impression and design my day's outcome.

I lingered there, among the sons and daughters, fathers and mothers, aunts, uncles, sisters and brothers, and forgotten child, where dreams are rarely realized and many are lost to wanting. Slowly, like picking apples, I collect only the ones that suited my mood, leaving the rest for future contemplation.

Then, retreating to my warm and dry solitude, I laid each out to examine, one before the next, it was at that moment, at that end of a journey taken, I found my inspiration to write about a Sunday rain.
just me and my conclusion.

Today It Rains

today it rains so many tears
reminders of discontent,
it seems to rain most everyday
where passion's drops are spent.

some are for starvation,
some imprisonment,
others rain for cruelty
or maybe love's lament.

I gather those that reach my heart,
I wish I could gather all,
but when it rains so many tears
my container seems so small.

I process these within my soul,
careful to wash them clean,
then spread them out to ones I love,
to quench their dried up dreams.

Wanderlust

the earth crumbles beneath my tread
announcing a new fixation upon
this once unbroken firmament.

branches of evergreen split the granite
backdrop in harmonious earthen tapestry,
I am drawn to a pause in over-growth.

golden shards penetrate the canopy,
showering light upon this announcement,
beauty everlasting fills my vision.

I am struck by knee buckling amazement,
my spirit retires to calm and tranquility,
I plant upon this my vision's gratitude.

this perfect place distils my reckoning,
cleansing me in worldly sorrow retreat,
I rejoice my unencumbered practicalities.

disturb not my lust for this serene sanctuary,
I capture a moment of creation and wonder,
is this the place where life began so long ago?

I breach the undisturbed stillness and
enter into this delicately arranged grove,
horizontal under stately pine I surrender.

my mind's eye reaches out with little effort
touching the tree tops then beyond,
I follow this journey to Heavens Gate.

My Listening Tree

confusion sometimes overwhelms me,
raining down in constant after thought,
leaving me unkempt, abysmal, scrutinized,
a feast for all lost and abandoned dreams.

misting up about me with cruel intention,
so undeniable, this taste of molten brine,
there is little left in the shallows
to appease these reckless apparitions.

this, however scorned upon my wreckage,
finds me searching for atonement and release,
though I walk this darkened path of decay
I have, save one avenue that guides my purpose.

most may find this the darkest place of all,
barren from winter's unforgiving torment,
yet I find solace, companionship, release,
it never fails to replenish my optimism.

My Listening Tree.

my wanderings occasionally produce a mortal
clarity so vivid, all else seems irrelevant,
such was the case on an early April morning,
as spring peeked around the corner.

I wonder, had it been any other day,
would I have fallen to such a spell,
had I chosen an alternate path, would
my world have been less affected.

would I now be writing of bitter hearts,
life challenges, or starry nights in June,
as it is, I'm caught in a memory I can't
release until I write it to conclusion.

the path, a downward incline, masked
in overgrowth in an attempt to dissuade,
unable to discourage my curiosity,
I breached this hideaway with a sense
of true discovery.

the morning haze hung like spectral angel
hair, wisps of whirling ethereal motion,
before me a garden, withered and unkempt,
as if painted on a canvas of abandonment.

tell-tale signs of once flourishing life,
undeniably elegant in pose and vision,
dried leaves carpet the earth in mosaic
design, their pattern shifting to breeze's whim.

A vine masked the west wall, speckled
in broad-leaf green, a final attempt to renew,
weeds stood victorious against the ravages
of some distant battle to dominate.

rose bushes bowed, defeated in varicose entrapment,

defiantly making their thorny presence known,
the twisted remains of a peach tree's limbs
reached skyward in pianist finger's plea.

three tulips survive in bell-shape petal contrast,
perhaps eager to lure a wandering
bee to pollinate, three white crosses stand
evenly placed in geometric fascination.

their marble, pitted by the ravages of time,
gothic statues against a forgotten facade,
at the base of center cross props an
ancient long-neck in translucent blue.

inlaid in the faded glass reads 1941,
below a jigsaw piece missing from it's base,
the morning sun reflects its blue haze,
striking the center tomb in azure brilliance.

I was left to wonder, is there some lost
hidden message here to decipher, these
three marble announcements, devoid of
any engravings, hold no answers.

tranquility overpowers trepidation,
wonderment replaces apprehension,
a moment so overpowering, I am sure
I have touched Heavens Gate.

visitation appears to be a rarity into such
a peaceful interlude, calm reaches in and
captures me, I can't help feeling angels
thrice smile down graciously and watch
over all who enter this amazement.

the joy which encompasses my trek back
stays with me long after I regain my day's regimen,
I decided never to return, for that moment,
in that place, would never repeat, nor should it.

I Thought of You Today

I thought of you today,
before sunrise,
my moment after slumber,
before day's challenge,
my time,
where I live truest,
bound by solitude.

I didn't think about
our conversations,
no,
I didn't think of what our friendship meant,
I know it seems eccentric,
why not friendship,
why not our bond?

there was nothing tied to it,
as though
it was meant to have meaning,
no,
not like that at all,
it wasn't some past moment shared,
it wasn't that at all.

it was you,
just you,
as you are,
who you are,
nothing more,
the simplest of truths,
you,
stripped of all history,
admiration,
judgment,
guilt,
reward.

a moment so pure,
as to say,
I shall never know loneliness
or how it must feel to stand in a desert,
it was you wrapped in purity.

Cricket Balladeer

if I fall between the cracks
to dance among the vermin,
slither slide among the creepies,
stir inside your hee-bie-gee-bie's.

dig in bones among debris,
live a life of shame yet free,
hear me play my concerto,
your cricket balladeer.

I see the worry in your eyes,
will he drone on through the night,
should you feel like joining in,
sing along and dance till dawn.

guard you well while you are sleeping,
from a corner thoughtful peeping,
protective eyes I cast upon you,
no one hurts you evermore.

if you hear me down below
and wonder how I'm doing,
rest assured you'll feel my praise,
your cricket balladeer.

Emily Waits

Emily paused above the harbor,
the sunset rusted evening calm,
she stood and took in its beauty,
each boat moored in harmony.

masts bob and weave to ocean's pulse,
facing a waning sun,
a graveyard of spent journeys,
the finality of yet another day's end.

in town nothing changes,
walkways overburdened with curios and souvenirs,
taverns and eateries bulging with party seekers,
sailors full of rum and tall tales.

cloud's ever changing pallet set against
pastel sunrises and marmalade sunsets,
never the same, indifferent to her boredom,
the openness of the sea paralyzing at times.

she felt her life slowly slipping through
her seventeen year old fingers, as with
most her age, a world of undiscovered
adventures seemingly just out of reach.

Emily can't help but wonder
if she might be the only one waiting,
waiting for destiny's rendezvous,
her romance still to be written,
waiting to join her mysterious captain
on some far away exotic treasure hunt,
waiting for true love to fell her, waiting still.

Caterpillar on Sill

alone is such a cruel word,
abandoned a truer tale,
left alone to discover a world
she knew so little about,
always an object, molded
formed and displayed,
bitterness an avenue easily taken
in the comfort of her past.

she sat on window sill
entwined in her thoughts,
cloaked in her rebellion,
the evening's calm of little comfort,
a lust to hurt at its zenith,
scarring her belief in conversion,
a caterpillar cursed, unable to transform,
unable to fly.

one thing she did understand
throughout her detachment,
this lover that brought her here,
could no longer score her,
his astringent touch would eventually
fade as would his taste,
his friends and family left behind
to empty reflection.

time passes too slowly,
deliberately one step turning to two,
at first there was no daylight,
just an outer shell of guilt,
thankful at times to be sealed
from the outside world,
chipping away at her inner fabric,
one day at a time.

pinholes at first,

glimpses of brighter days,
always returning to long
vacillating self doubt,
gathering strength,
attacking with proclamation,
she stands, at this moment
without hesitation.

I am woman,
perfection from within,
I am new, radiant,
full to overflowing,
my wings are my curiosity,
my colors are many,
my resolve undeniable,
I can hate, love, cry, and laugh.

the walls suddenly turn
true in color,
the horizon emblazoned
new beginnings,
her body supple and radiant,
without blemish,
she sees for the first time
her transformation.

Big Yellow

the pale moon hangs low like yoyo unstrung,
only tree's silhouette interrupts my appraisal,
an autumn lunar announcement set free,
filling the night in overbearing neon.
Big Yellow!

tides flung against man made interruptions,
erosions lost in time only to be resurrected,
I stand out in reflection, my silhouette reminding
me how daylight's shadow respond's to my quest.
Big Yellow!

masked in solar desire, I sacrifice my madness,
gather up my astonishment amid life's peril,
if it's me, then it's truly me who collects the
autumn wind, I accept my place among these
ever changing retreats.
Big Yellow!

I am molded from earth and accepted by nature,
calm overtakes my bundled anxiety as I achieve
Big Yellow!

Backstreet Avenue

sparse streetlights glow,
their condensed perimeter
giving way to periods of dark
foreboding spells of loneliness.

slight glimpses of failed dreams
catch the rain passing through
each beam as if to wash away
each broken promise's reflection.

the tarmac whispers brighter days,
its sheen caught in secondary reflection,
gutter river flow gives motion where
stillness has tried choking resilience.

a single traffic light at the far reaches
announces stop, go, slow as if to beleaguer
the cycle of life, slow, stop, go in radiant
color bursts filling a peaceful night.

a lone breed interrupts the calm, sulking,
head low, hunger overwhelming despair,
hunting curb to curb, in zigzag affair,
a deliberate ritual lost to repetition.

with each turning leaf fall holds
fast its grip and daylight struggles
to pierce her emptiness.

crystal beaded dew scatters across
her valley as yesterday bleeds into
memory.

understanding comes with its usual
sacrifice, her heart unwilling to find
calm and reassurance.

she sits on balcony's edge awaiting
dawn's reconciliation, the starling
beckons her change of mood.

release this dagger left in the wake
of love's betrayal, find her a new
heart pumping new life.

blue sky melt her recent tragedy,
that she may face another crippling
black night.

sleep no longer a comfort realized
for night's the enemy, a shadow
wrought with should have been.

I sit at measured distance, suppressing
my uncompromising desire to ease her
sorrow.

I count the days until her awakening,
only then shall I stand before her and
ask her to love again.

2

I often wonder what lies beyond my safe haven,
am I fortunate or lost in mediocrity?

Beyond the Blue Door

he knows his life
and what he'll be,
tattoos paint his loyalty,
no diploma, no degree,
his father died at thirty-three.

four kids she has
one on the way,
a crystal pipe to
light her way,
caught in a life she
won't betray,
her savior must have lost his way.

justice drives an Escalade,
pistols strapped
to insure all pay,
he must be God,
he's not afraid,
fear he feeds on everyday.

their gospel written
on prison walls,
to stay alive
one must walk tall,
they may get out, should
they get the call,
societies brand guarantee's their fall.

go find a job
in the land of the free,
minimum wage
supports his family,
you ain't part of this society,
you're cancer ignored in reality.

the media looks

but turns away,
precious ratings
they must not waste,
tell your children
they'll have to wait,
a celebrity's life to rehabilitate.

El Cantina

the desert holds a bitter heart
returned within pastel retreat,
inward out to lie about,
stretched out to limit's scale.

a sundown lantern shown in depth,
specters dance amid it's nest,
glowing soft an ember's blaze,
push closer warm despair.

chiseled shards address the wind,
to lose the gain then back again,
purity the whistling breeze,
fractured drifts this wanting.

closer now to center's gate,
break the bonds adrift in fear,
gather up the courage rare,
progression's quake retaliate.

sit and rest thy weary thought,
drink the light that warms a heart,
dance to merriment divine,
then off again in life's pursuit.

Jelly 2

I rarely betray my inner voice knowing full well
it's my only trusted confidant, in lesser times I
wouldn't have given such scribbling a second glance,
but for reasons still unknown it captured me.

pasted on a bathroom wall of a rundown
service station, between nowhere and roads end,
was a farewell message of redemption written
in Sharpie black for all to devour and hypothesize.

To anyone who might stumble upon these words,

born into a ragtag band of wanderers
I was dealt the moniker "Jelly"
(no last name),
it was impossible to determine my heritage
from such an array of free love spirits.

spiteful as it may seem to some,
I grew to accept, even respect,
my surroundings and lifestyle,
given it was all I knew or understood
of a life given to adventure.

I do not regret living hand to mouth,
always on the move, never cultivating roots,
we are dealt our hand at birth and
design our destiny by the decisions made.

by my 15th year I was an outlaw having
killed twice to survive, you won't find
an apology for deeds against mankind here,
we do what we must to survive another day.

I am trapped in this rundown hellhole,
surrounded by law enforcers who would
just as soon kill this blight on society

as to bother with rehabilitation.

so, by no means will I leave here alive,
I ask of you a simple gesture, when next
you see what you perceive to be a
vagabond, you find it in your heart to stop,

listen with your heart and help if
you can, possibly, you will save a life,
please, do this for me, so I won't
feel my life forgotten to misdeeds.

design your life with this decision,
helping others less fortunate than yourself,
you may all find yourselves in Old Jelly's
shoes sometime in your ever-changing life.

Thank you, Jelly

well, needless to say, I was stunned,
I walked out that door with a new outlook,
indeed, it left me with a sense of clarity
undiscovered prior to this epiphany.

from that day forward I was Jelly 2,
for I was the vagabond he had written
about, changing my name required
no more than a pronouncement,

because I am just another of societies
forgotten, so with duffle bag in hand
and a bounce in my step I headed out
for places unknown and adventures
yet discovered.

Thank you,
Jelly 2

Perfect Garden in the Sun

in a garden stood three flowers
displayed in color harmony,
to the eye all may seem perfect,
perfect garden tranquility.

One is tall as Sunday morning,
head held high in regal pose,
pride is blinding One's compassion,
bow before One's perfect world.

Two has greed to fuel its wanting,
breaking vows to fill its need,
justifies Two's power turncoat
by the seeds the others sew.

Three is easily persuaded,
does not question actions done,
rides upon one single purpose,
follows blindly anyone.

One will have all he desires,
Two will take and not return,
Three will whistle all is perfect,
perfect garden in the sun.

One decides Two isn't worthy,
Two is busy exploiting Three,
Three still whistles all is perfect,
perfect garden in the sun.

Two wants more than Three can offer,
Two sees One could fill his need,
Three still whistles all is perfect,
perfect garden in the sun.

One says bow before my beauty,
One must quell Two's lusted greed,

Three still whistles all is perfect,
perfect garden in the sun.

lashing out Two ends One's power,
Two has nothing quenching needs,
Three still whistles all is perfect,
perfect garden in the sun.

One's false pride has caused his downfall,
transparent greed Two's bitter end,
Three must follow without question,
Perfect garden in the sun.

One and Two succumb to dying,
flounders three with setting sun,
no more singing in the dawning,
perfect garden's reign undone.

In a Castle

in a castle lives a maiden
no one sees her anymore,
wrapped within her tragic scandal,
bars of guilt cast on her door.

once she lived a life of wonder,
dancing on her crystal floor,
all were caught up in her magic,
spinning dreams upon life's shore.

then one day he struck her fancy,
dressed in black this troubadour,
singing songs of love and heartbreak,
captured heart forevermore.

once he cast his spell upon her
she was added to his score,
taken from her virgin flower,
left her wanting at her door.

left to drift within her shadow,
shaded veil to stain love's light,
no more magic only sorrow,
lonely cries her deepest night.

in a castle lives a maiden
no one sees her anymore,
wrapped within her tragic scandal,
bars of guilt cast on her door.

My Wonder

I am left with little more than wonder,
to the naked eye this may suffice,
I however deserve more, for I need to
understand and digest to believe.

I stand on mountain top,
surveying all that is given,
is gratitude enough to complete me,
should I be happily ignorant.

no, I fear my collage of dysfunction
finds me momentary, happily ever
after crippling my desire,
I lust to walk among freethinkers.

I think me not alone, if so then
I am solitary, but as with most
living things, a gathering holds
more than desire.

yes, I believe it worthy to step off,
fly among eagles, run with the leopard,
learn from peers, as they alone can teach,
then may wonder find me complete.

Sadie, What Have You Done

occasionally I go back,
back before now, back after then,
a place charged by emotion,
the silent majority's awakens,
a fork in the road, if you will.

Volkswagens and Woody's
painted in psychedelic frenzy,
sunflowers, morning glories
long hair, laid back, tuned out,
turned on, acoustic rebellion.

Alice through the looking glass,
the Age of Aquarius, the sunshine
of our love. dead heads, moody blues,
Huxley's journey through the cosmos
a toke, a hit, a buzz, reefer madness.

back to the summer of love,
the summer of a thousand dances,
tie die and paisley, Janis to Creedence,
peace, love, Motown, Woodstock,
Suite: Judy Blue Eyes.

the infancy of a revolution,
demonstrations on Capital steps,
politics charged to frenzied riots
blood soaked campuses and southern
streets, human rights the coming storm.

soldiers fighting a cause long forgot,
citizens fleeing to foreign lands,
Old Glory in flames of effigy,
a President, a Profit, a Senator,
martyrs of a land opposed to change.

a band in search of enlightenment

returns from a Far East hiatus,
The Walrus, disillusioned, begs
"Sexy Sadie, what have you done?
you made a fool of everyone" *

* a quote from The Beatle's "Sexy Sadie" written by John
Lennon

Mariners Blues

walk with me to waters edge,
oh hear the mariners blues,
of families torn asunder,
a fragile heart to lose.

tales of gallant heroes,
tales of love gone wrong,
tales of battles won and lost,
tales told with a song.

let us dance and sing this night
on beaches soft as clay,
of ships long journey recompense
where buried treasures lay.

oh sorrow of the mariners
that sleep on ocean's bed,
dance with me among the fog
and quell the hearts long dead.

My Familiar
(depression's reign)

I walk the distance in solitary confinement,
toppling my crippled reasoning,
sprouting cannonade's flaming mist,
covert sirens appear
haunting my emptiness.

I watch as vultures gather overhead,
iconic vacillating broods circling my despair,
suffocating layers stack up about me,
sealed by pearl-covered casket latches.

strip me of desire's overwhelming grasp,
pressing down my undersized conclusion,
spewing gutter soaked guilt without regard,
I cut like warm butter, heel like damaged goods.

attack, fade, then attack again,
continuously reforming,
only to crush my confidence,
rebuilt from caution's past,
torment the now and then,
just dust from long forgotten overtures.

daylight once again flung against me,
washing my guilt clean and pure,
another challenge hangs in the distance,
patiently loitering just out of reach.

my armor returns as moments repeat,
days turn to weeks,
my goals strengthen,
I am battle hardened,
a testament to my fortitude,
my uncompromising will.

Ibby Krump

No one knew when Ibby Krump decided he could fly.
While I don't believe it matters, non-the-less, it is a
curiosity. Most people paid little attention to him and
found him an embarrassment to their small tight knit
community. You would find him walking the streets
muttering in conference with his many internal voices.
He has always been different and possibly a little
invisible at times. I find myself wondering what
passes through his complex and driven psychosis.
Does he relate to his exterior world or is it just grey
matter.

evil one I feel you here
designed to paranoia's web,
do you taste a bit of triumph,
twisting dagger knows remorse.

Ibby held in foolish conquest,
blind ambition not much more,
throws aside any compassion,
crippled in a crippling world.

step by step he gathers visions,
battles demons at his door,
turpitude not in his morals,
pacified by voices scorned.

spreads his wings for far off places,
not confined within his soul,
eyes must gaze the abstract presence
of external specter's war.

fly this world you hold inside you,
sore upon reclusive shore,
take in all your haunting remnants,
happily ever after more,

I think all townships have been acquainted with Ibby Krump, in one form or other. We pass him on our streets and contort our gaze in ignorance or go out of our way to avoid him. Are the Ibby Krumps of this world, somehow, aligned to a deeper purpose? Do they exist to test our karma? Do they deserve our apathy? I take pause to wonder, and then move on as though my day is undisturbed.

The Isle of O'Dauley

I walk along the shores of O'Dauley
where all lost battles reside,
I morn lost heroes,
their cries of injustice,
asking to clarify their sacrifice.

I hear them taunting the wind,
was I able to change man's hunger,
they cry out in defining measure,
did I fight the last battle of lost empires
in over-powering transgression.

I fall silent,
I haven't the answer needed
to quench their quilt,
their desperate need.

I embrace their long
forgotten battlefields,
they did not ask for war,
I honor their branded bravery,
reconcile all faulted palisades.

I turn upward announcing my disdain,
the pious thrones that delivered them
unto this blood stained holy land of
worn-out pledges, misguided platitudes.

I weep for the masses lost,
my tears turn to molten lava
upon this firmament,
with each drop
another welcomed into Valhalla,
I strike with open palm
the affluence that deserted them.

on bended knee I beg forgiveness,

I pledge never to forget
and promise with heart wide open
to walk beside future generations
and share my influence.

my heroes, my saviors, my friends
never to be forgotten, forever grateful.

Own It

I happened on the news today
and was shocked by what I saw,
causing me to think out loud,
in fractal ins and outs.

a child died in her mother's arms,
desperation robbed a liquor store,
thirty-eight died in desert raid,
under weather bright and warm.

Darfur was never mentioned,
nor the elderly left to starve,
someone mentioned fashion sense
like they turned on some alarm.

I watched a nameless plan hatch
by a generation past its prime,
with eyes wide shut and reckless,
destined to repeat their crimes.

I learned to make spaghetti
while lobbyists pay to win,
maybe I'll move to Italy
so these laws can't box me in.

but I take heart in knowing,
when I wake up everyday,
that honesty and peace of mind
is how I get my pay.

When you're Silent
   (to save my heart)

I am thrown headlong into my endeavors,
at times,
I risk it all for passion's sake,
when I am moved,
I have no failsafe,
what then,
if not stirred by controversy.

find me not of fragile porcelain,
judge me,
as I lust judgment,
I carry my banners high,
with them,
my unwavering dignity.

if you see me less than eye to eye
announce your opinion,
I am not without flaw,
you without sway,
I a student of life,
as are you.

I wound like any other,
your opinion may tarnish this armor,
however,
without your rebellion,
I am but an empty glass.

challenge is not the aggressor,
ignorance the dragon I fear,
if we find level ground,
rest assured,
I'll stand with you until we prevail.

speak up for I am listening.

A Fish out of Water
(a hero's return)

marching footstep's echo
the palpable anticipation of
air raids and incoming,
daily routines once familiar
now empty shells,
so difficult to let go.

the barracks stands empty,
all that remains are memories,
unique bonds made in combat,
the fallen never to return,
the wounded, their course
forever altered.

friends of the deepest commitment
dispersed to far off destinations,
promises of lifetime contact
so abstract in contemplation,
names disjointed in a new reality,
collections of imagery locked away.

afraid of being left behind,
a hometown lingers frozen in time,
loved ones and family now foreign,
painful memories, a promise once, now
married with children, old love
letters worn and faded.

the door closes as another opens,
a hero must return to life's ritual,
alone, without guidance or regulation,
stripped of childhood dreams, a reality
that has forgotten his sacrifice so easily.

Rubber Man

I fell once, it seems so long
ago, thinking back, it was
recent, I don't feel crippled,
maybe, I never landed.

I felt a September rain,
an awakening sending me
reeling inward, or
did I simply consider it so,
never questioning, just reacting.

my design still holds fast,
my vision unobscured,
undaunted in my pursuits,
single-minded of purpose.

I am who I have always been,
though I may seem obtuse,
forgotten to grander schemes,
still, I feel flexible, buoyant.

no matter, as with so many things,
this will pass into emptiness,
I learned long before my fall,
time keeps us resilient.

Empty Cobbler

his pock marked digits,
like brail, revealing a life time
of dedication and love of labor.

he counts the remaining yards,
as though his finest leather could,
somehow, recover happier days.

these days, he questions his ability
with each patient stitch, doubt, a
ghostly guest refusing to leave.

remembering he once fitted the
affluent that now steels his
livelihood with mass imitation.

his craft beaten by a world
of disposable goods, tearing at him,
leaving a wisp of his former.

approaching his easy chair that steels
his purpose little by little, he draws
from blood read Pinot.

he sits remembering past years
of repair and resole, the cushion
which granted him creativity.

he will languish in lost desire,
slowly turning to stone cold,
waiting for darkness to appease.

his devoted wife, try as she must,
wonders when a shallow future
will finally overtake optimism.

she knits to knit, anything to dull

her bruised heart caused by the
wilting of a once proud man.

impatiently they await tomorrow
if only to escape today.

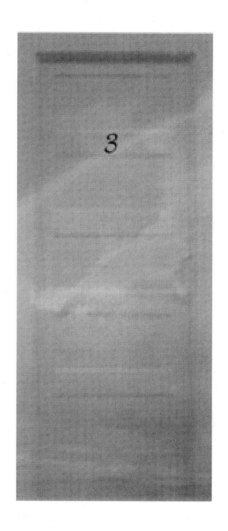

3

if our illusions become our failures then we are destined to criticize their outcome

Talk to Trees

talk to trees,
point to leaves,
bring back the
slow moving sunshine.

drive fast,
make it last,
no one knows
where you've been.

move with direction,
trip with aggression,
hop up and down, then
see who joins in.

wish without a star,
toast life's confusion,
walk the altered path,
life begins within you.

talk to trees,
point to leaves,
bring back the
slow moving sunshine.

The Butter Knife

the versatile butter knife,
a somewhat curious utensil,
spreading butter efficiently
is remarkable unto itself.

dig deep the creamy peanut butter,
surely more than you'll need,
dress your toast, your cracker,
your finely carved celery stick.

a finely crafted tool
for all things condiment,
thinly veiled mustard spread upon
your burger masterpiece,

I relish the taste of a ballpark frank,
so expertly laden,
a mix of alien preparations.

but, oh, you argue with alacrity,
everyone knows these common usages,
barely a reason to waste a page,
but let us dissect this miracle further.

a screw driver of undaunted proportion,
a pry bar to the task of ruination,
a press for the pill too large to swallow,
a scraper to remove a substance
long since spilled.

I could go on but you capture my drift,
such a finely tuned apparatus
yet so simplistic in nature,
I venture to say the one
claiming this invention
was a genius of the first magnitude.

Apples to Oranges

some statements in life become
nothing more than an announcement,
the truer message lost to interpretation.

let us examine a long standing
rebuttal which stands the test of time,
rarely succumbing to conclusion.

to get to the heart of one such confutation
let us peel away the layers to arrive at
the very core of this misguided affirmation.

"You're comparing apples to oranges."

in order to resurrect its truer message
I offer you this in depth assessment.

picked from the bough, the apple is
easily washed and devoured, however,
the orange demands meticulous preparation.

extricating the rind,
a ritual only enjoyed by purists,
 requires a perfected skill,
making certain to remove all that remains

of the white follicles which stick
stubbornly to the delicate inner skin,
while cracking the code that
produces the bite sized wedges.

orange juice, a staple of any breakfast table,
apple juice, apple cider, apple sauce
let's never forget a staple of Americana,
the infamous apple pie.

here, the apple trumps with variety,

cider, a concoction that rivaling
the finest wine,
nothing dresses a feast
like a fine sauce.

extracting a fair amount of juice
gives new meaning to the phrase,
a bushel and a peck, I dare say
Mr. Appleseed should praise our ingenuity.

it's hard to imagine an orange fritter yet
consider apple juice, grenadine and tequila
how so very unappealing to the pallet.

now that we've examined the pros and cons,
albeit, the differences of such nectarious bliss,
we must take pause to reflect and discern.
in conclusion let's not forget one important
consideration, had Eve so boldly
picked an orange on that fateful day
a need to argue
may never have been necessary.

If I Had Monkeys
(in my backyard)

if I had monkeys in my backyard,
I dare say what it could mean,
I'd have to warn the neighborhood
and buy some signs for all to heed.

I'd buy bananas by the bushel
and plant some coconut trees,
I'd grow those vines that Tarzan used
so they could swing for me.

maybe by a Toucan
so they would feel at home,
to make them look presentable
I'd buy a monkey comb.

I'd play a hurdy-gurdy
so they could dance and sing,
I'd have to charge admission
but kids would enter free.

some neighbors aren't as friendly
as I wish that they could be,
but when the monkeys rode my bike,
they'd all come out to see.

I could mix a batch of my favorite tea,
serve those cookies that I love,
I'm sure in time it would break the ice,
and we would have some fun

I'd have to let them in at night
if it snowed and turned real cold,
give them all some monkey treats
if they did what they were told.

I'm sure there'd be a lot of things

if I thought about it more,
that they could do around the house,
maybe learn to do the chores

laundry, dishes, make pizza pie,
just to name a few
maybe they would be the ones
in Oz who could fly too.

oh joy, what fun and merriment
as we joined in sing-a-long
don't forget to bring a smile,
if I had monkeys in my backyard.

Still Life

a rundown cabin long forgot
of musty air and wooded rot,
accessed by primordial door,
collapsed and cast upon the floor.

a chandelier that never shines,
whispering wind to move its tines,
a mortared place of mosaic stone,
rusted grate of iron bone.

a piece of cord emboldened knot
dangling from a rusted pot,
coffee can of random toss
in musty blanket tepid moss.

a cowbell sits in dust collected
upon a foot stool long neglected,
scraping heard by resident rats,
seen through walls of piney slats.

a cupboard door no longer red,
spider's lair at center web,
a counter top once useful place,
formica peel upon its face.

a one eyed doll sits in one corner
waiting for forgotten owner,
a children's glee lost to the wind,
never to return again.

a relic falls in timeless trance,
forgotten lives, forgotten dance,
a place abandoned long ago,
of family ties that couldn't grow.

Rodents Three

in a pipe under the shed,
three rodents spend their day,
when evening settles into night
they scurry out to play.

they know a tiny whole somewhere,
a secret passageway,
I can hear them in the cupboards,
when my stuff gets in their way.

I decided to buy a trusted trap
and lure them with some cheese,
but all I had was cheddar sharp,
they're Swiss mice, if you please.

I asked the butchers daughter,
could she help me with my plight,
she said they don't sell rodent,
so she's not sure what was right.

I went to Mr. Dibbledap
and told him of my fix,
he loaned me his cat Mighty Max
who would hunt them, just for kicks.

one hour in the house alone,
I was sure that this would do,
but when I went to check on him,
he was playing a kazoo.

Three Blind Mice his chosen song,
as the mice danced the Finny-Mac-Dee,
now you may think this would set me off
but I joined the dance with glee.

now, I set four plates for dinner,
one man size just for me,

the other three are tiny,
but I let them eat for free.

the moral to this story,
if there is one to believe,
judging strangers at first glance,
is the wrong philosophy.

The Bench

I walked across the bridge today,
a park bench my final destination,
first, taking in my familiar surroundings,
I relieved myself of a day of shopping
and prepared to devour a new novel.

a young couple, occupying a bench in proximity,
I would say of teenage category,
switched to a whisper as we exchange smiles,
a giggle or two concerning, I can
only surmise, our obvious age disparity.

Mrs. Applebee claims her usual spot,
much like a box seat at the ballet,
entranced by the ongoing performance
of pigeons vying for her attention,
Mr. Applebee long since passing.

Jake and Taylor here every day,
playing checkers win or loose,
always a collage of onlookers,
a Rockwell constantly changing
as the days shadows lengthened.

you, sitting there taking in the world,
soaking in all life has to offer,
new to our parade of onlookers,
just passing through? just on this day?
his expression giving way to suspicion.

while the trees dance and billow
to their own private serenade,
I hesitate before returning to print,
for I have discovered the tempting
yet elusive perfect day on the bench.

Bottleneck

rollin, tumblin' rhythm rumblin',
century aged like fine Muscatel,
locomotion rhythm, drifting riff,
layered in slam, shuffle, slam.

wrap me in your boxcar blue,
of heart pumpin, chest thumpin,
mind tippin', rainbow simplicity.

journey in your Delta dreams,
bottleneck slide night train bliss,
stompin' kicks, in a barefoot beat,
branded by the chain gang's shackle.

sing to me in toothless splendor,
cold hearted love and blistered passion,
suffer in your blue steel moments
at the end of heated barrel's finality.

preach to me of blues man wonders,
seasoned facial peaks and valleys, laid
out in jailhouse graffiti, scarred adversity
and desperate longing.

sell your soul to play at crossroad's sunset,
spit in the eye of the devil, blues man,
he won't have your rhythm soul,
your blues belongs at heavens gate.

God gave us you to suffer our sins,
let us smile at adversity, and praise your gift,
thank you, bottleneck blues man,
stand tall and sing your everlasting glory.

Carousels

I could state the obvious,
how life is like a carousel,
a never ending circle full
of ups and downs,
a metaphor for topics
too numerous to engage,
explored by poets and
fabulists throughout the ages,
I dare say it's all been captured by the best.

possibly, evoking imagery
of long lost adventures,
a knight on trusty steed chasing his nemesis,
chariots in heated competition
thundering across an imaginary finish line,
a damsel riding across a flowering meadow,
accompanied by her prince,
taming a sea horse in pursuit
of a long lost Atlantis.

perhaps a kaleidoscope of flashing abstract,
a dream collage of lights pulsating to calliope's
merriment,
songs perched on infants wonderment,
yet, so familiar to parents
caught in their child's role-play,
how a carousel is a child's journey into fantasy,
a glimpse into how the world might be,
frozen in time,
spinning ever forward,
oblivious to their soon contagious future.

But what I really came to announce is,
"I believe in Carousels"

do not be quick to judge or underestimate
the value of a life committed to solitary task,
all are here to serve a higher purpose, the
result defines each journey's worth.

to illustrate this pontification,
I call upon the little known,
yet highly regarded,
wood sprite,
in the hierarchy of the sprite community,
they are considered drones,
assigned an important task
claiming little glory in the offing.

trees, as we are all aware, are stationary,
only moving skyward,
it would seem to most,
a lonely and unfulfilled existence,
one would then be left to surmise,
if these knotty, yet majestic,
monuments were able to communicate,
it would remain within their tightly knit grove.

but venturing deeper,
we realize a purpose
undiscovered by most mortals,
the lowly wood sprite
carries an enormous responsibility,
in small villages peppered
throughout every forest, big and small, lives these
delightful,
well mannered sprites,
most living two to three hundred years.

here in lies the wonderment,
each tree relies on a wood sprite,
each wood sprite assigned a tree,

ingenious in simplicity.

when a tree holds a message to impart,
love for another,
news within the forest,
gossip, life discoveries,
philosophy, sadness, betrayal,
emotions of any sort.

the wood sprites sole purpose in life
is to relay these messages to all other trees,
bouncing around the forest,
rarely seeming to rest,
always true to their message,
what a divine journey indeed.

so if, upon your walks in forest green,
you happen to cross over into fairy world,
as sometimes happens,
be careful not to waylay
this marvolous messanger,
for their journey's worth is of truest nature,
not to be defined in mere mortal terms.

A Black Widow's Legacy
(the male's perspective)

my destiny holds little mystery,
my fate is understood,
 I need not sort out deeper meanings
for my purpose is well defined.

the cycle of life spread out before me
in easy to understand
paint by numbers ideology,
in order for future generations
to exist, my sacrifice, essential.

I suppose to less courageous species,
this philosophy may seem ambiguous,
yet in my mind, what better legacy
may one impart.

what possibly, could be gained
by hiding in the shadows,
living out my life until old
age overtakes me,
my mark on life never realized.

loss of life, surely a tragedy, does
not effect my expectation,
nor will I resign myself
to survival of the fittest,
in some foreboding cavern.

I don't feel it, a life lost to
undiscovered possibilities,
this sacrificial lover welcomes
destiny openly and without fear.

Loss

there's a dollar on the sidewalk
found by a poor lost man,
he's been hungry now,
this week gone past,
no one to fill his hand.

who's the widow in the kitchen,
sadness painted on her face,
it's the child without a mother
lost without a trace.

the poor boy who will never know
the father who lost his way,
so he grows into a bitter man,
then finds he cannot stay.

a woman who can offer love
but hides it deep inside,
the evil hand that strikes,
is the ghost that took her pride.

I think of all the loss I feel,
it takes a hold of me,
like the loss I've felt
in the ones I love,
no-way to set them free

as I travel in a world of doubt,
most happy people turn away,
because they know a step away,
is their loss that hasn't found it's way.

Spaghetti Cowboy

as the sun beats down
on parched grasslands,
a ghostly image appears,
above the horizon,
in heated ripple distortion,
a silhouette's deliberate approach
leisurely takes shape.

a melodic theme, seamlessly,
gathers strength,
holding all eyes upon
this pale rider's approach,
his past lives left to
hopeful imagination,
while isolation surrounds
an iconic specter.

living outside the law
of a lawless land,
relegated to righting wrongs,
aiding the underprivileged,
the down trodden,
a hint of Robin Hood
and Zorro hidden below the surface.

in his countenance lives a
million I told you so's,
yet, answers escape him,
redemption his last reward,
solitude his final apology,
captured in life's haste.

a celluloid son, born from
forgotten old west pandering,
riding steadily towards sunset,
call in your markers my forgotten hero,
and Hang Em High.

Pinky's Pink

much can be said of Pinky McNair,
not least of which is her pink, pink hair.

most people say she wants it that way,
truth be told, it just gets in the way.

her best friend Misty told her to change,
black or blue or a cool red hairdo.

Pinky exclaimed, in her usual tone, if you
don't like my look then leave me alone.

still the question remained in head,
what would change, if she changed to red.

so she picked up a mix, with a wish to
let go, then teased it and wheezed it
into a fro.

she stared her reflection but couldn't
decide, flipping and flopping with
feelings inside.

this just wouldn't do, she thought deep
inside, so she hid in the closet until
the red died.

she's pink once again and happier too
after all she is Pinky and vowed to be true.

The 13th Chapter

I hide within the page's mass, separating the former from the present. Descending in exquisite challenge, I vow to carry this journey to its conclusion. Was it chapter three that spread me thin? Drifting in character seeds, tempting me to skip ahead and live more quickly in its content. What price must be paid to alter my recognition? Gloom and doom doest grip me, holding fast my senses. My right and wrong drips upon this measured plot, drifting once more into an undefined truth. Then snap with recoil abandon back into an altered manifest.

If true to these words, a reckoning hides at journey's end and will surely lift this vale of secrecy. New to my discoveries, character flaws twist me in spiral decent of murderous betrayal. My hero, my chosen one, now holds guilt at the end of a tattered noose. Panic grips me in the cold hands of deceit. Chapter 13 now spread out before me. My hypothesis stripped clean, revealing my hindrance to conclude. Slow, methodic, the last pages reveal little yet my loyalty stands in opposition to compromise. I pause to reflect, jigsaw pieces fall one by one accelerating my senses. Bells chime somewhere unknown and go unanswered, as I smile in recognition. All is revealed, my hero lives triumphant, promising to sleuth some future volume.

The End

Cabin Corners

I didn't consider leaving overnight,
this thought had slowly and deliberately
crept into my consciousness, given to
many nights of reliving past memories.

the picture above the mantle,
painted long ago by a distant lover,
relives a sailboat battling turbulent
water, still stirs my adventurous side.

an easy chair molded by years
of restful contemplation and
authors, spinning tales upon
bound numbered pages.

a bookshelf's permanent inset,
ghost branded in skyline stains,
triggers memories of lonely dirge,
when Koontz and King held me fast.

a pair of butcher-block lamps
illuminating a threadbare chesterfield,
its necessity abandoned to unrequited
lust, held by transparent engagements.

the kitchen sink, stainless, displays
a window of amateur design, framing
my garden, now lost to overgrowth,
where ghosts till my forgotten pandemonium.

each item reminders of a life
that no longer holds my interest ,
I could go on but what purpose
could nostalgia possibly serve.

memories flood over me in
an attempt to discourage,

this, of course, expected for
loss always predetermines change.

a surreal sense of accomplishment
now draped in dust cloth disguise,
I exit through the kitchen door,
lock my past away and move on.

Full Moon Feast

wide awake over covers peeping,
seize me not this full moon feast,
walls have eyes to search within me,
fear doest chill me to the bone.

shadows lurk in every corner,
whispers carry to the wind,
phantom glance descends upon me,
ghostly white this mirror mask.

remind me not past resident torture,
branches dance through window's pane,
darkened halls of hardwood creaking,
night train beckons all-aboard.

toss and turn a black cat weeping,
distant shutter grip gale's whim,
chimes the bell that steals the hour,
save this soul from specter's hold.

haunt me not these evil minions,
Gideon's book cast to the floor,
disregard my lost transgressions,
can repentance make me whole.

hear my pledge which echoes softly,
from this day and evermore,
I will vow a better person,
future cast my just reward.

counted sheep now gather around me,
calm reclaims my shaken soul,
full moon feast retires its warning,
redemption's promise fades with time.

*the definition of turmoil is the difference
between love lost and love found*

A Woman's Love

"there is nothing more profound than a woman's
love"

a baby's life blood, a young man's arbitrator,
a daughter's foundation, a lover's release,
a light far beyond the darkest reasoning.

she may never choose who to love,
she loves according to her design,
unconditional like water finding level ground.

a love so pure, even betrayal cannot shake it,
the perfect creation treated as an object,
instead of a gift freely and completely given.

defined by the lineage that precedes her,
we as mere mortal men can only accept,
unable to understand the depth her love embodies.

to all that touch my life I pledge my soul,
no matter how desperate life becomes,
I will forever hold you in special light.

to all that abuse this love, I have only
pity and contempt, for you will never
stand in her glory or measure up to her gift.

Angel Song

I do not know from where it comes,
igniting light to bring the dawn,
I dream of misting island's shore,
waves of clear blue ocean mood.

my past regrets seem distant reach,
a knight on stead, a jester's glint,
instant flame from heart's reproach,
beyond dark region's road.

I know not why it comes to me,
this precious vision's vast degree,
if I could ride on flowing wave,
what homeland spawn her fair.

it's me that makes her vision real,
it's me this fantasy repent,
to her I bow and patience ask,
her angel song my wanting need.

The Last Piece

as days sift through life's hourglass,
the urgency to become more than I am
sometimes overtakes the more important
things in life.

why must I damage the influences
in my life, the parts that give life
purpose and meaning, I know not this
person I have become.

when I pause, I realize, I am running,
running from life's challenge,
running from
the very things that shape me.

why, at this time in my life,
I am not who I aspire to be
leaves less to speculation
and more to reasoning.

now, I am laid out in jigsaw,
all the pieces, save one, are
in place, the last a perfected
fit, I place acceptance and smile.

A Rose Sacrificed

a rose is cut from thorny stem,
special in nature,
gathered or alone.

few demanding,
few unselfish yet
contrite if without purpose.

a statement,
message to message,
hand to hand,
life to life.

purity unconditional,
sometimes wielded,
others accepted,
embraced to heart.

complex yet simple,
bold yet subtle,
benign yet poignant,
free yet demanding.

each unique in stature,
each created bond,
each a message,
journey to destination.

so begins the sacrifice,
redemption delivered,
given as love, yet secondary
without emotion.

to this end, give thanks,
for few things heal
so completely as
a rose sacrificed.

I Am Here

I cast upon my simple word,
spinning, circling, unknowing,
find a heart to linger in
vast Spirit Sea of wanting.

bring her here upon my lyric,
hold back nothing messenger,
relate to me in distant longing,
I too feel in lost and found.

fly my desire, my wanting,
my impatient transparent touch,
reprisal taunts my recognition,
eternal dust in truth affected.

I stand before your spirit,
I strip all pretence clean,
find me not a crumbling tower,
for I am here and you are not.

Each Thought of You

if I could love myself
as I love you,
I would step off this
higher promise,
deepest commitment,
purest emotion,
without a second thought,
never a regret,
just spinning,
tumbling in honesty,
expanding my world,
with each thought of you.

Poor Little Sista

internet princess,
sucked up in a vacuum,
will she find a love that's real?
lookin' for a soul mate,
tryin' out a fresh date,
feelin' like she got the raw deal.

Tom, Dick or Henry,
could have made her happy,
little things just lost to appeal,
is it any wonder,
she won't invest the time,
to find out if he is the real deal.

why oh why,
can't she see past the surface,
why oh why,
are they all to blame,
why oh why,
they're all a bunch of losers,
why oh why,
where are the richest with fame.

drivin in a black bug,
eating up the radio,
never really knowin how to feel,
when life is such a tragedy,
and everyone's so lame,
all the little sista's feel the same.

poor little sista,
sittin in her bedroom,
wishin all her dreams could be real,
lookin in the mirror,
dredging up the past,
searchin for another life to steal.

Attempted Cool

I was not surprised in the least,
it was as if he had always known,
maybe, that's why she felt indifferent,
just a passer by hoping for a nod.

I must admit, he was nervous,
I knew he had but one attempt
at her guarded, yet welcoming heart,
in this situation, rejection an all
too familiar design.

I was sure it of his own weave,
I'm guessing of course, but I would
brand him overstated, even overly
reckless, in situations such as this.

my opinion would hold him needy,
uncontrolled, and overbearing by most
standards, marking his territory like
a paranoid shepherd, not that others
would hold him in contempt.

some would agree its all hit and miss,
but this was new, unused, just a look,
so inviting pulling at his heart, so perfect
as to write its own ending.

I knew this smile reflected in his eyes,
poised in front of him, like a wisp of spring,
wasn't obtuse, from my vantage point the
sun's rise and fall would profit greatly.

this was of beauty yet discovered,
warm, tender, innocence in translation,
like touching the sky at daybreak,
this his life altering moment, indeed.

the words stalled at the edge of decree,
his palms turned to used up flypaper,
his pulse betraying a wish to calm,
his thoughts a whirlpool

the moment quickens as he felt
her slip through my hands,
"Can you dance"?
what did he say?
crushing him to sunder,
enemy voice.

"I...I....mean Will you dance?"

"with me, damn" he whispered,
oblivion pounced, sucking the
life from the room.

he tried recovering then he heard
"yes"
in the echoing distance

my son's first dance turned,
just as it should, I smiled and
left him to his night to remember.

Chelsea on a String

dancing, spinning by request
a damsel in despair,
guided by a clever soul,
parades her everywhere.

caught within his selfish wanting,
stuck within a cannon shell,
severe strings that binds desire,
let her loose then make her well.

many dreams have passed before her,
a captured heart has been betrayed,
her rivalry paints desperation
upon a canvas heart facade.

cut her loose you puppet master,
your presence shames her poisoned
heart, fill your empty mind with
purpose. free her from this mental bond

Chelsea on a string,
dance little darling dance,
caught up in imagining,
her life a raging trance.

Chelsea on a string,
no one could ever know,
why her love is tied to him,
now she fades in afterglow.

Passage Way

apart from this,
away from that,
I cast a curious eye.
away from that,
apart from this,
darkness when I try.

gone from me,
without you,
a lonely place to be.
without you,
gone from me,
this our destiny.

I live a life,
as do you,
upon a desolate road.
as do you,
I live a life,
of future tales untold.

walk with me,
I'll walk with you,
together we will be.
I'll walk with you,
walk with me,
caught in our gravity.

Hourglass

you are hourglass,
every moment, every day,
my past sifts through your
simple life and reflected calm.

your silhouette transfixes me,
against your sliding door,
a full length slip clings to your hip,
you turn, I loose control.

you are hourglass in burgundy,
and earrings of small pearl,
hair that lightly frames your nape,
you are woman, deepest desire.

sweetheart of my morning,
change my whispers into song,
melt away my caustic thoughts,
hold me in your careless arms.

Upon Return
  (no way out)

        she lays on feather bed,
        lost to spent passion,
        the afterglow still burns at her core,
        once again, alone in her thoughts,
        his promise of love so strong at first,
        so sure of his commitment to her.

        he has taken, once again then discarded,
        in her heart she is not surprised,
        played out in past enactments,
        in his mind he has gifted her
        sure she is the fortunate one.

        this time, as times before,
        she vows to end her downward
        spiral, never again to be his trophy,
        even while these words take shape,
        she understands her strength will fade.

        he will return when he finds no other,
        returning to quell his lust to dominate,
        she wonders if the pain and despair he
        leaves in his wake is well planned
        or is he so shallow of conscience.

        like a dog marking his territory,
        his cruel passion lingers,
        unable to let go she holds his lust,
        inhaling his scent that stains her,
        even now her longing grows stronger.

The Calling

she stands against the wind,
waves at furies end
lapping at her feet

her hair in keeping with the gale,
transparent gown billowing
in lucid waves of silken white.

the sun relinquishes its grip,
at days end she calls out

"I require this void be gone."

she casts her love like fishing net,
finished with her loneliness,
strengthened by her longing,
never to return.

with sunset reflected in her eyes,
she challenges the wind,
palms extended, her bare feet
clutching the sand.

"return my love, as it is given,
return with last attempt,
for I am here on Donegal Shore."

"my place of places,
my haven heart,
my harbinger,
join me, to live and love."

an empty heart awakes at sunset's end
answering her call

Intermission

no one seemed to notice,
exciting my inner senses,
I take you in, file it away
for future reflection.

holding back your comment,
you feel invisible, understated,
it shows in your demeanor,
maybe, a meant to be moment.

never judging, yet contemplating,
caught in your haven of ambiguity,
your masquerade of self-doubt,
capricious, is not what I read.

your silence, a protective cocoon,
passing through the crowd,
a specter unchallenged,
perfected by the simplest glance.

I pause to take in your beauty,
should we return, your lips parted,
yes sweetheart, I whisper, your
moment passes, my heart trembles.

as we sit down awaiting Act II
my smile is one of admiration,
as the curtain draws open
you touch me and I swell.

Candle by the Bed

patiently alone, undisturbed,
light me so I may dance across
your wall, let my serenity cover
your emblazoned crust.

loose yourself within my aroma
therapy, release your passion swell,
I do not mind,
I want your secrecy,
I cherish your heated breathing,
share your wandering touch.

read from impassioned tomb,
that I may light your word,
let me reflect within your reading glass,
capturing your warmth to return.

use me, shape me,
strengthen my inner core,
I am the calm that will never abandon you,
in time of crisis or wanton heart.

hold me up,
walk with me,
I long for your gentle grip,
in return,
I promise to lighten your mood.

My Captain, Your Heart

I wonder through these shorter days,
should I be one of happy endings?

it sometimes seems my percentage weakens,
left in the rain to fend against the torrent.

like a lost sailor at sea,
my compass mists over.

must I gamble at every turn,
should I feel every bump?

am I rational or confused,
I feel your lantern held high.

you wait, like me, forever in the wings,
it's hard to judge your grand gestures.

still, it must be said,
you hide it well,
a cloak, a vale of illusion.

my confidence is a house of cards,
my wishes scattered by the gale.

destined to repeat the easy mistakes
this sprinkler forever caught on return

I do, however, stand at your bow,
checking for land mines lost at sea.

we travel so fast it's difficult to prepare,
every hope becomes my failure.

I pick through the scraps with every encounter,
our choices just leftover attrition.

the ones, important to others,
hope, desire, fulfillment steer us true.

my captain, your heart.

My Longing

I cast upon my simple word,
spinning, circling yet unknown,
find a heart to linger in,
vast spirit sea of wanting.

bring her here upon my lyric,
hold back nothing messenger,
relate to me in distant longing,
I too feel in lost and found.

fly my desire, my wanting,
my impatient transparent touch,
reprisal taunts my recognition,
eternal dust in truth affected.

I stand before your spirit,
stripping all pretence clean,
find me not a crumbling tower,
for I am here and you are not.

Puddle Jumping

I find myself at the far reaches of life's absolutes,
where complications hold little more than irritation
and dreams, more times than not, miss their objective.

drifting among uncertainties, resembling
dusty rungs on a tattered ladder, I live life simple,
nothing premeditated, my grit has long been tested.

I jump from frame to frame, cull to cull, never
returning
to a life unresolved, leaping within my outlying
reflection
where tidal waves of regret find little curiosity.

for I have learned to drape my allegiance in
life's proven truths, only the simplest
of statutes survive the test of time.

I do not hide from life's disappointments. I, my
friend,
have found a place of wonder where all is possible
and discovery but a puddle away.

He stood from a rather tiring discussion concerning the pros and cons of being in a relationship. Leaving his companions to discovery. Lifted by three glasses of red, he walked to the front entrance. Thankful to be alone, he pushed against the door as the daylight washed over him. His squint trying to adjust as Fleetwood Mac faded in the background. Familiar with his surroundings, he chose a path. His cursory manner not of purpose, it's that nothing held him slower.

Surrounded by graveyard, he stalls for air as his eyes capture the single flower. Four petals of yellow held in stark contrast against a background of marble memoriam. He takes in the shear tenacity of the lone flower and the simplicity displayed by the four petals. Encroaching upon this peaceful domain, he moves to stand before the headstone. Scribed within its marble face, as if to speak to the world, he reads.

IN LOVING MEMORY
REMAINS
DAYNE PURCELL
1955 – 1993

FOUR PETALS I GAVE TO MY ONE TRUE LOVE
THE DAY BEFORE MY PASSING
EACH WITH SPECIAL PURPOSE HELD
A SIMBOL OF LOVE EVERLASTING.

ONE I GAVE IN GRATITUDE
ONE PETAL FOR MY HEART
HOLD THESE ALWAYS CLOSE TO YOU
AS YOU LEARN TO TRAVEL ON

ONE IS FOR YOUR FUTURE WIFE
SO SHE KNOWS THAT I APPROVE
AND FOR YOUR CHILD AS YET CONCIEVED

THE LAST I GIVE MY LOVE

FOR ALL WHO PASS WITHIN THIS GATE
THAT HAVE NEVER KNOWN SUCH LOVE
PLEASE TAKE A PETAL SPAREINGLY
FROM THE FLOWER GROWN OUT FRONT

ONE THING MORE BEFORE TRAVELLING ON
YOU MAY WANT TO KNOW HOW IT'S DONE
YOU MUST GIVE YOUR HEART UNCONDITIONALLY
BEFORE YOU MAY FIND YOUR TRUE LOVE ONE

Clutching the four petals in his jacket pocket he pauses for a moment thinking of new beginnings. He bends down holding back his emotions and kisses the headstone. He then turned with little reluctance and gazed out into a world undiscovered. He takes the first ceremonial step and enters a new life.

Young Love

gather before me all my past loves,
teach me once again, dissect,
examine, and release sensibility,
languish at the surface.

why must I compare compatible beauty,
to my past conquests, nay apparitions,
dispense judgment blind emotion,
dismiss all that fail to conform.

will I walk down lost roads,
only to choose a safer road
the road my former constructed,
will the alternative hold a greener
blade.

I am new, unpredictable and disarming
the mirror holds an older, wiser reflection,
the weight of my past keeps me grounded,
I am certain I once soared among my fancies.

I must fly again, beyond the familiar,
feel the fresh breeze of passion,
challenge debilitating remorse,
feel once again the pastures of young love.

Sanctuary

if you believe in sunshine
as I believe in rain,
we could walk together
halfway in-between.

you must believe in lightning
for I'm your thunder man.
enhancing all your well intensions,
if you'll take my hand.

can you find our differences
appealing to your mood,
or am I incandescent,
a fool to fall too soon.

are our paths so different
that well intentions lost,
within your grace I'll find a place,
caught upon your pause.

I place my thought upon you,
outside this pristine flaw,
await your drifting judgment
of passion unresolved.

do you feel the ripple
that travels on your tide.
or is my sanctuary just
a place for us to hide.

Pain Sublime

there is lyric in the wind,
can you hear, no, not of
empty words, weighted
contemplations
closer...closer.

they're right before us,
passing so quickly yet
lingering for eternity,
their ripples mark us.

beyond.... beyond,
out past the far reaches,
touching forgotten places,
in understated boomerang.

catch me alone somewhere,
lost within your calm,
whispers are but our echoes.
statements of crumbling praise.

tiny and unassuming
like a thief's repentance,
pause with me then,
repeat the unbreakable cycle.

nothing of life holds such urgency,
our future masked in our past
moments, this time we are
every word, every pause.

every exclamation beckoning
to reach out farther now,
closer, touch my urgency so
I may cherish your response.

I shatter like late breaking news,

if only I could stay, although
absence is a tortured understanding
where pain is pain sublime.

Stand in My Light

I suppose lingering
outside your heart
could be misconstrued

desperate, certainly not,
foolish, I don't mind,
stalker, I will not stay.

can we love if not loved?
can we dance if alone?
can we admire from a distance?

stand in my light,
drink from my cup,
see with my eyes,

now tell me,
do I love in vain
or love too much.

you would know
you, so loved by many,
so afraid to love again.....

Missed Opportunity

she passed into memory
like a slow moving cloud,
what was once heartache
now a starved emotion.

if only I could replay
this missed opportunity,
to recapture this chance happening
and awaken my passion anew.

if I must live without,
then wipe my thoughts clean,
find in me the toggle,
the switch to release.

must I live out my life
in could have been,
sleep comes willingly.
dreams choose their path.

A Critical Touch

> what inspires one,
> walking an unknown path,
> a maze of half-truths,
> temptations and fears,
> to discover their true
> destination and hold onto
> their integrity and self-worth?
>
> what inspires one,
> under extreme odds,
> when all seems forgotten,
> when darkness falls
> like a suffocating blanket,
> to reach out into the abyss
> and hold onto some
> semblance of self?
>
> what inspires anyone
> to lookout into a world
> driven by greed and deceit,
> hunger and poverty,
> to stand above all piers,
> and shout-out.
> I can make a better world?
>
> maybe, I say,
> it's not what, but whom.....

*"by no means are these the only inspirations, however, these
are prime examples of how a single spark can ignite a
firestorm."*
with your permission, jdr

myspace: http://www.myspace.com/jdroland
website: http://jdroland.webs.com/
email: jdroland@msn.com

look for JD Roland's future books
"curriousities, oddities, and arrangements"
coming fall of 2008

~

"The Apocalypse Diary"
coming in the spring of 2009

a look into humanities obsession with overcoming fear
by conquering those of dissimilar beliefs, makeup, ethics,
and religion through poetry and pros.

the journal of Avery Johnston,
a simple man that survives the end of civilization
as we understand it.

this book promises to be an experience in
content, format, and imagination of
unique proportion.

jdr
never the end
just a new beginning